What does God want me to do with my life?

Steve Swanson

AUGSBURG Publishing House • Minneapolis

WHAT DOES GOD WANT ME TO DO WITH MY LIFE?

Copyright © 1979 Augsburg Publishing House

Library of Congress Catalog Card No. 79-50086

International Standard Book No. 0-8066-1722-5

Photos: Jean-Claude Lejeune, page 6; Jeanne Hammond, 20; Rick Smolan, 27, 59, 62, 72, 84; Paul Conklin, 30, 48; Camerique, 40; Freda Leinwand, 81, 94.

Permission to quote from *Gift from the Sea,* copyright 1955 and 1975 by Anne Morrow Lindbergh, has been granted by Pantheon Books, a Division of Random House, Inc. Permission to quote from "Surrender as the Noble Course" by Andrew M. Greeley has been granted by the author.

Scripture quotations unless otherwise noted are from the Revised Standard Version of the Bible, copyright 1946, 1952, and 1971 by the Division of Christian Education of the National Council of Churches. KJV stands for King James Version.

MANUFACTURED IN THE UNITED STATES OF AMERICA

To my parents—
and to all Christian parents
who struggle to guide their children
toward a rich future.

CONTENTS

INTRODUCTION

Mary Laurence walked into Pastor Anderson's office, trying to manage a polite smile. When she sat down, she began to cry. Pastor Anderson waited a minute, then pulled out a desk drawer to get her a Kleenex. "What's bothering you, Mary?" he asked. He expected trouble at home, or maybe some sexual hang-up.

Mary's answer both relieved and challenged him. "Pastor Anderson," she said, "I don't know what to do with my life."

Mary was upset because so many people had so many different plans for her life. Her grandmother wanted her to be a missionary, her mother hoped she would be a teacher, her father hinted she should be a lawyer, and Jerry wanted her to be a housewife. Although she didn't realize it yet, she had come to Pastor Anderson to find out what God wanted her to do. As they talked, it would seem to Mary that her pastor kept asking what *she* wanted to do.

Mary was not the only teenager in Forestburg who talked to Pastor Anderson about vocation and life work. Even though the high school had two vocational counselors who had lots of training and lots of books about how to choose a school or profession or job, there were still many Marys around who didn't know what to do with their lives.

Mary's concern was deepened because she was a Christian. She wanted to do the right thing. Christians, she thought, should really want to know how to spend their lives, and especially young Christians, who hadn't wasted half their lives already. Mary wanted to do it right the first time, so she went to her church, to her pastor, to get some answers.

As Pastor Anderson thought about Mary's concern, he knew what he wanted to get across. He wanted to tell her that the church has always had some things to say about vocation, about God's plans for people's lives. He felt like starting from the beginning with the creation story and how we are spiritual beings, created in God's image, made of the same spiritual stuff as God is. He wanted to tell Mary that God gives us life and being, time and energy, so the challenge is to use that life, that time, that energy in ways that will please God.

But Pastor Anderson knew that if he said these things they would sound like a sermon. He could see Mary was in no mood for a sermon. Instead, he would explore with Mary her needs, her aptitudes, her dreams—maybe some of her weaknesses and hang-ups, too.

He knew that finally, though, a girl like Mary

wouldn't be satisfied with anything less than the greatest challenge of all, the challenge of Jesus himself. In the end, "What am I going to do with my life?" would come down to a focus on small acts of service and love. "Whoever would be great among you must be your servant, and whoever would be first among you must be your slave" (Matt. 20:26-27).

Pastor Anderson would say to Mary, "God wants you to be a servant." He knew that her next question would be, "But how?"

This book explores some of the "hows" for Mary and for other young Christians as well.

WHO IS THE REAL ME ?

Pastor Anderson didn't think "How?" was the next question at all, even after Mary asked it. "You'll never know how to be a servant unless you first learn who you are. Ask yourself, 'Who am I? Who is the real me?' "

"That's partly why I've been upset. It's not so much that I'm nobody, although I feel that way sometimes. Mostly it's that I'm so many different people."

"What kinds of people?"

"Well, it's like Grandma Laurence wanting me to be a missionary. Remember last year when that missionary doctor spoke to us—what was her name?"

"Lydia Johnson."

"Yeah. Well, I thought about her being a doctor and helping all those sick people in Africa. For a while after that I wanted to be a missionary doctor. I was doing pretty well in French, very well, actually. The real me is good in languages. I like to help people, too. Why couldn't I be like Lydia Johnson?"

"What about Jerry?"

"If I were like Lydia Johnson, I wouldn't get married, ever. That's another side of me. Some days I want to be a wife and mother, and some days I don't. I like little kids—it's fun to baby-sit. And I like being with Jerry. I'd like to live with him. But then he says something dumb, or my folks get into a big hassle. Then I think it would be nice not to get married at all. Do you know what I wanted to be when I was in junior high?"

"No, what?"

"A nun."

Pastor Anderson smiled. He remembered another Mary, Sister Raymond Mary, who'd been in some of his classes in graduate school. She was so smart and so gentle at the same time. He wanted to tell Mary Laurence about Sister Mary, but he knew that was off the track. "You gave up wanting to be a nun?"

Mary nodded. "Mainly because we don't have them in our church."

"Let's get back to Lydia Johnson, then," Pastor Anderson said. "Would you be a missionary doctor for your grandma and because you wouldn't have to get married and because you're good at languages?"

"No, I couldn't. I don't think I could leave my family for that long. Besides, I'm not so good at science, and doctors need that. And you know what else? I like *things* too much. To be a missionary would mean giving up our nice house and

11

car, a bath whenever I need it, an electric hair dryer. . . ."

"Don't sell yourself short," Pastor Anderson said firmly. "You'll be surprised at some of the things you will do without when you really get wrapped up in your work or study, or your marriage. But let's see now. You have said some things about the real you." Pastor Anderson began ticking them off on his fingers. "Liking languages means liking to study, and you care about your church, and you want to help people, and your family means a lot to you—hassles and all—and you like little kids." He looked up at Mary. "Who else are you?"

Mary seemed to have come to a dead end. She couldn't see any other sides of herself at all. After a minute, the pastor said, "Imagine that you're in a house of mirrors and everywhere you look is a reflection of you. Imagine each reflection is different. On five of those mirrors we can already see you as a student, a church woman, a missionary, a family person, a wife and mother. Can you see other images of yourself?"

Mary thought for a while. "Well," she laughed, "once I wanted to be a movie star, but I gave that up in grade school."

"Let's go back to baby-sitting. That's something you *do*. You learn things about yourself by doing. What else have you done?"

"I tried skiing last year with Jerry. I found out it isn't as easy as it looks. And I found out something else, too—I don't like Jerry or anyone else telling me what to do. We got into a real argument that day."

"Maybe that's why your dad sees you as a lawyer, when you argue."

"I'm a mean arguer." Mary smiled.

"You're independent."

"That's it. That wouldn't be so good for a nun, would it?"

"Not really, no. What else have you tried?"

"I've always liked traveling. I like to go other places—but I like to come back home, too."

"Maybe we don't have to extend the list any more. You are already many things, Mary, and each time you try something new you'll learn more about yourself. Don't be afraid to try new things, and above all, don't be afraid to fail. You learned some important truths about yourself when you tried skiing."

"And if I keep trying to do things, I'll know myself, the real me?"

"You'll know yourself much better, and when you do, you'll know better what you want to do."

Mary nodded, but she wasn't satisfied. She could have had this same conversation with the counselors at school. Pastor Anderson had shown her some ways to discover what she wanted, but there was a bigger question, a more frightening question: What does God want me to do?

2

WHAT DOES GOD WANT ME TO DO ?

Mary asked the question out loud: "How can I know what God wants me to do?"

Pastor Anderson thought about that one for a minute. He remembered many times in his own life when he wasn't sure whether he was going God's way. He knew how difficult this question was, and how serious it was for Mary.

"Mary," he said, "what are the ways we can learn things about God? How does God communicate with us?"

"The Bible, certainly," she said, "and the church."

"Yes. Any more?"

"People like you. People who work for the church. We learn about God from you."

"Yes, that's part of my job. Your Sunday school teachers have helped you, too, over the years. Any others?"

"Other people, especially Christians."

"That's true," said Pastor Anderson, "but your

mom and dad and Grandma Laurence are Christians. They're trying to tell you what to do, but they're each telling you something different, and you aren't accepting it."

"I know that. What I think, though, is that when Granny wants me to be a missionary, it's her will and not God's will. If I did her will and not God's will, wouldn't I mess it up?"

"You probably would. I've known several pastors who have done just that. They went into the ministry to please their parents. All but one of them has left the ministry for other work. It's important that what *you* want to do and what God wants you to do work together somehow."

"That's exactly what I was thinking," Mary said. "But if I can't trust the people who care about me, who can I trust? Maybe even you could give me bad advice."

"Sure I could. As a matter of fact, when I was younger I think I urged a couple boys toward the seminary mainly because it was what *I* wanted them to do. But let's get back to what God wants. You said that God speaks to us through the Bible, the church, and other people," he said, raising up one after another of the fingers on his right hand. "Any others?" He was pushing back his little finger in anticipation of a fourth source.

"I can't think of any."

"Prayer," he said, squeezing his little finger hard.

"Of course!" she said. "I've been praying almost every day that God will show me what to do. But sometimes I don't feel much different after I've prayed than before."

"It's that way with me, too, sometimes. But when we pray, we register our concerns with God. I think that makes a difference to him. If we care enough to pray about it, God will make a special effort to answer those prayers. Sometimes the answers come from the Bible, the church, and other people, just like you said, but most often God answers back right through your own head. He helps you *know* what you really should do."

"You mean *know,* really know for sure?"

"Yes, I mean exactly that," Pastor Anderson said emphatically.

"Do you know you're doing God's will by being a pastor?"

"I do now. I know for sure, now. I didn't for a long time, though. But I went on working and praying and thinking about it—and considering other work. Finally God got through to me that I was right where I belonged."

"And you think it will work like that with me, too?" Mary asked.

"It may. It often does. We're all different, though. Sometimes it's easier for God to speak to us by saying yes, and sometimes he has to say no."

"What do you mean by that?"

"Well, let's say God wants me to be a pastor, but I want to be a nuclear physicist. Maybe I overlook the fact that I'm not so good at math, but God doesn't overlook it. I start out on a physics program in college, but before long I fail calculus. That's God's way of saying no to nuclear physics. I can't go on in physics without calculus, so I have to look elsewhere for a vocation. God may have to

16

shut one or two more doors, but sooner or later I'm headed for the seminary and for the ministry, just like he intends—unless I shut out his will entirely."

"You mean a person could do that?"

"Sure, and plenty of people do. It's only temporary for Christians, though. We make wrong choices, but God lets us know soon enough. Most of the time God provides a way to use even the wrong choices. They give us experience and insights we can use later. We see God's will best when we look back. I can look back for years and see God's hand in most of my choices."

"But I can't look back that far," Mary said. "How can I see God's will?"

"There's plenty to see, even at your age." Pastor Anderson started listing on his fingers again. "Consider that you were born into a Christian home, you are a daughter of the church, you are getting a good high school education, you live in a nation where you don't have to be what your parents were, you have a variety of choices for education or training." He changed hands, ready to extend his list to number six. Instead he swept his finger across the whole hand. "The list could go on and on. You've had many advantages, and you've already made many choices. God's will has been in it from the beginning."

"That may be true, but what am I going to do next? That's what bothers me."

"What do you want to do?"

"I think I want to go to college, but I don't know where to go or what to study—and it's so expensive."

"But maybe that's what God is saying to you, even if you aren't sure about it all. We can only take one step at a time. Maybe when God gets you to college, he'll give you more direction."

"How could I know that?" Mary asked.

"You'll probably only know for sure many years from now as you look back."

"But what about the other things I might do instead?"

"Would going to college right away keep you from doing other things later—being a missionary or a lawyer, or getting a job, or even getting married?"

"I guess not, except maybe getting married. What if I meet someone I like better than Jerry at college?"

"You wouldn't want to marry Jerry this summer if there's someone better waiting for you, would you? Jerry wouldn't want that either."

"No, I guess not. But I can't imagine anyone better than Jerry."

"If God wants you to marry Jerry, then going to college first won't change anything. Maybe you'll be more sure if you wait."

"Maybe so. You think then that I should go to college?" Mary, feeling fairly satisfied, was shuffling around, getting ready to leave.

"That seems to be what *you* think, and that's probably what you should do. Can we pray before you go?" Mary nodded. "God, you guide our lives in so many ways. Guide and direct your servant, Mary Laurence. Help her to see more clearly the paths you have laid out before her. Give her faith and courage to make bold and sensible decisions, knowing that you intend her life to be satisfying and good. Keep her close to you as she lives through these exciting, frightening years, for we pray in Jesus' name. Amen."

COLLEGE: NOW OR NEVER ?

Late in his senior year, Mark Hanson shocked his parents by saying, "I'm going to hitchhike to Montana this summer and get a job in a mine."

His mother and father were disappointed. Mark had been accepted by two colleges, and they'd been sure he would choose the one they had gone to. He didn't choose either of them. He wanted to work, and he wanted to ski, and he wanted to be independent for a while.

Kathy Benton seemed to be giving up her plans to go to the university to study microbiology. Her friend Beth told her about an inexpensive course in operating business machines, and she decided to register for it. She wanted to get a job in an office, earn some money, and be on her own. Her mother tried to understand, but her father didn't even try. He was furious.

When Scott Elstad graduated, instead of going

to the police academy as he had planned, he took a job with the highway department. He held stop signs for a repair crew; he was a stick man for a surveyor; he drove a pickup truck that set out orange cones behind a line-painting crew. His mother was so upset when he started the job that she wouldn't talk to him for a week.

Three years later, Mark, Kathy, and Scott are all back in their parents' good graces. Mark is a second-semester freshman at his parents' college. Kathy is at the university. She uses her business-machine skills to earn part of her tuition, working in the biology department office. Scott never became a police officer, but now his mother brags to her friends that he's at the institute of technology studying traffic management.

Mark, Kathy, and Scott are three of hundreds and thousands of young people who postpone college, university, or other training for a while and make it work to their advantage. Instead of disregarding their wanderlust and their qualms, as many students did in the 1950s, many of today's graduating seniors are trying other things before going on to school. They are working, traveling, staying at home. They are taking short vocational-technical training courses so they can work at better-paying part-time jobs during the years they're in college and during the summers in between. They're bumming around, doing free-lance artwork, playing in small-city orchestras, acting for experimental theaters for no pay at all.

Not all of them come out quite as well as Mark, Kathy, and Scott. Some of them learn there's danger in staying out of school for more than a year or two. They may get excited about their jobs and the money they earn. They may begin to think they should make careers out of their first jobs. (And maybe some of them should, who knows?) They may get established and comfortable, finding it easy to be at home in their own communities. They may fall in love and decide to get married.

Many middle-aged men and women who made these kinds of choices years ago are now getting back on those long-unused tracks. Their kids are grown up and gone, or at least in school all day, and that gives them time to retrain and to make realities out of the dreams they set aside years before. It is usually harder than it would have been if they'd pursued their dreams sooner.

Alice Carnes found that out. She went back to college when her youngest girl started high school. Although she had plenty of adult experiences to draw on, she found it hard to compete with young students. She also discovered that much of the terminology in math and chemistry had changed since her school days.

When should *you* start college? Are you a Mark, a Kathy, a Scott? Will you become an Alice? You should not start until you are ready. Most academic counselors suggest, though, that you be ready by the third year after high school. Otherwise, if you're much older or more mature than most of your classmates, you'll have trouble relating to them as social equals and lose out on the rich and rewarding social side of college.

John Mulligan was in the marines for four years before he started college. He really likes the school and his classes, but he moved out of the freshman dormitory after only one month. "They all seem like my kid brothers," he said.

Postponing your college entrance beyond two years may be a threat, not only to your enjoyment of campus life, but to your ever starting at all. Many students who have just finished high school have built up a certain momentum during their senior year. In spite of being very tired when the school year ends, in spite of all the final exams and the cramming, in spite of the emotional shredding they go through in leaving friends and sports and activities behind—in spite of it all, they discover that mentally they are still students.

They may have been studying harder than ever before. They may have been in the thick of the scholastic life, the social life, the athletics, the music, the activities—everything that high school has to offer. They have loved it, the studying and the student life, the whole works. For them it is probably best not to break that momentum.

If you are among those who discover they're still students when they finish high school, you should go right on, stay with it, and start college immediately in the fall term after high school. Don't let anything stop you—not money, not the good summer job (". . . and they want me to stay on next year"), not your sweetheart, not your fears and anxieties—not anything. If you're ready to go, go!

WHERE SHOULD I GO ?

If you decide to go to college, your next question will be, "Where should I go?"

Your decision will be partly made for you if you have fairly definite vocational plans, particularly if those plans involve very specialized training. Noel, our middle son, wants to study paleontology —rocks with fossils and such. There are only a couple of schools on the American continent that offer such a program. That narrows his choice considerably. Programs such as architecture or engineering, astronomy or nursing, are available only at universities or technical institutes. You may simply have to go where your program is offered.

On the other hand, many students like Mary Laurence don't know what they want to do with their lives. Most college freshmen and sophomores—and many juniors and seniors—haven't yet chosen a career, but they're busy exploring possibilities in their general liberal arts programs.

There are at least a dozen good colleges that

offer liberal arts programs within 50 miles of our front door. Few Americans are more than 50 miles from a college. If you expand that 50 miles up and down and across this continent, there are literally thousands of choices. Maybe you wonder, "How can I choose the right college for me from among all those thousands?"

You can eliminate many options by choosing first between the church college and the state college or university. For general liberal arts courses, there is often little difference between the small church and state colleges. In state and church schools of comparable size, the choice of courses and instructors might be about the same, the subject matter studied very similar, and the performance level expected about the same. In every area, however, there will be schools easier and harder, prestige schools as well as small, relatively unknown schools—some of them very good indeed. The demands and levels of competition among these schools may vary widely.

The large state university is a special case. It is apt to have the biggest and best of everything. That is both good and bad. Introductory courses in most departments may involve very large lecture sections, but often there are excellent lectures by big name professors.

Judy Dolan came home from the university at Thanksgiving with stories of a history class with 500 students. She reported that no one seemed to know or care whether she came to class or not. She heard some lectures live and some from a can of videotape, and some were televised. The actual teaching was done by graduate students about five years older than she. She said they seemed inexperienced, although some were eager and engaging, pretty good teachers, really. One of her teaching assistants, though, was ineffective and hard to understand.

Judy figured she'd be in her third year at the university before she escaped teaching assistants. By then she hoped to get into classes and seminars with the teachers everyone raved about. They might even recognize her when they met her on campus. Judy thought learning from them would be exciting, and she decided that was worth waiting for—even three years.

Malcolm Page went to St. Andrews college. He usually got into small classes taught by regular faculty members. His freshman English section

was actually taught by the chairman of the department. So even in introductory courses, Malcolm was on a one-to-one basis with some of the most experienced teachers on campus.

Choosing between the large university and the small college is sometimes difficult. Each has its advantages. If you decide a small college makes sense, then you have to decide between a Christian and a secular school.

There are some fairly large satellite colleges connected with state universities, but most Christian liberal arts colleges are quite small, from 500 to 3000 students. The smaller the school, the more involved a student is apt to become in extracurricular activities and in the social life of the school. Malcolm was so busy just before Christmas that he barely got ready for finals.

In smaller schools, students are likely to get personal attention when they ask for it, and sometimes even when they don't. Malcolm didn't ask Professor Larson for advice, but he got it anyway. "You're too busy," Larson said. "You're letting your classwork slip."

The main reason more young Christians don't attend church colleges is that they seem more expensive. The basic tuition fees at a good church college may be from 25 to 50% higher than at a comparable state school. The total cost is often not much different, though. Basic tuition appears to be low in most state schools, but it may not include many of the costs. Special fees are often tacked on later: library fee, activity fee, etc. Add to that some high rent and food costs in the metropolitan areas where most universities are. Then add transportation costs. You may find that the price of a state-school education may be nearly as high as that of a church college.

All good colleges and universities have financial-aid programs. If you want to attend a church school and you're accepted by its admissions officers, you should be able to work out the finances through the financial-aid office.

You and your parents will have to decide whether the extra cost of a church college is worth it. Many parents say yes. They know church-college campuses are by no means the havens of angels some people wish they were, but they think exposure to Christian teachers and students, many of whom are from their own denomination, is worth a great deal. Many also see advantages in being among others of similar economic and cultural backgrounds, who share similar values and moral views. The chances of choosing a mate while in college are up to 85%. Being with a higher percentage of those who share similar beliefs and aspirations on a church-college campus is of more than passing importance.

5

CAN I LEAVE HIGH SCHOOL BEHIND ?

Many students don't make it in college because they can't or won't leave high school behind. Sure, high school is fun and you may well cry real tears on graduation day. But high school is only one stage in your educational and social development.

When Mary told Pastor Anderson how much she would miss high school, he asked, "Would you really want to stay in high school for 25 years? Can you imagine your Grandma Laurence as a high school cheerleader?" Mary laughed.

College is different from high school, partly because of who is there and why. High school is the last phase of public education, the last unit of "required" popular schooling. Almost everyone in a given town or a city neighborhood goes to the same high school. High school solidifies community feelings, the sense of belonging to a town or neighborhood. When Mary goes back home years later, she will recognize family names and maybe say to a gas station owner, "I went to school with your sister," or to a carry-out boy, "I'll bet I know your father."

Certainly if you go off to college, you shouldn't cut yourself off from your hometown roots, nor should you develop a snobby sense of superiority over high school friends who aren't attending college. Nevertheless, when you leave for college, you should leave certain ideas, attitudes, and relationships behind.

One big high school idea to leave behind is that education is free. It has never been free. In grade school through high school, buildings, books, and teachers all cost money. All the townspeople pay, whether they have children in school or not. You may remember your father moaning about high real-estate taxes. Much of that money goes to local schools.

A college education is even less free. It requires a large outlay of money. Unless your parents are wealthy, they will probably have to do some head scratching to figure out the finances. Working with the college financial-aid office, they will try to put together work, loans, government grants, and money from home into a fund large enough to swing at least one year of college.

College tuition and fees are direct payments. You and your parents will pay monthly, quarterly, or semiannually for room, board, and tuition at college, and it will be a major investment. But even at that, your fees cover only part of the cost. Taxes, government grants (more taxes), business and corporate grants (part of everyone's cost of living), and alumni gifts often pay for one-third to one-half of the cost of education, even at a private college.

You should resolve from the outset to make the best possible use of this investment in your future. Because higher education is so expensive, and because other people are paying for part of it, your vocation as a student, your calling while in college, is to be the best scholar you can possibly be.

A second high school attitude to leave behind is that teachers are enemies. That feeling may go back to kindergarten and first grade, when somehow your mother was replaced by a teacher, an authority figure you didn't automatically love, who didn't automatically love you in return. She (I use the feminine deliberately) may have been a loving person, but perhaps she seemed to love all the children equally and therefore made you feel much less special than you felt at home.

In junior high and high school, perhaps some teachers seemed mainly interested in making everyone fit in and obey the rules. Getting along meant not making waves, learning predigested material and then handing it back on tests and essays. The teacher became the enemy.

It's true that some high school teachers fit that role quite snugly. There are also a few enemies teaching at the college level. They see students as clay to be molded to their own specifications. They persist in giving objective tests based on lectures from 20-year-old, dog-eared notes. Freshmen hear about them from other students before they even register for their first set of courses. Such enemies are to be avoided like liver a la mode.

But good college professors, like good high school teachers, are colearners. They teach, yes, but they also learn from their students. If students come to conclusions different from theirs, they will be eager to know about it. If students contradict them with good arguments and solid information, good teachers not only offer in return high grades, they accept such students as colleagues in learning.

Furthermore, college teachers have a stake in their students' success. Your college fees are in part direct payments to the men and women standing in front of your classes. You pay them to teach you. They want you to succeed as a student. They want you to get what they have to offer. That's how *they* succeed.

No college student should ever—and I can't emphasize this enough—feel shy or guilty about asking professors for extra help. Part of their job is to keep office hours to confer with and help students. The minute you have trouble understanding a professor or begin to fall behind in class, go up to him or her after class and say, "I think I need some extra help."

A third high school attitude to leave behind is that someone else is responsible for getting you up, getting you to class, and counting your nose after you get there. You will be far less regimented and regulated in college. About half of your professors won't even take roll. They figure it's up to you to get there and learn what they have to teach, even at 8:00 a.m. You will be free to go to class or to sleep in.

Malcolm Page sat down with his calculator one

day and figured his cost per class hour. He paid about $4000 for his first year of college and expected to take 10 semester courses during that year. Therefore, each course was costing him $400. A semester course meets about 18 weeks, maybe three times a week. That's 54 hours of instruction for $400, or about $7.40 per lecture.

Malcolm admitted that the $4000 also covered room and board, and he had to eat and sleep even when he wasn't at college. But he also figured that, in addition to $4000 in fees, college cost him an additional $4000 or more in lost salary, so he doubled his cost-per-hour figure. He guessed that if he had paid $15 for a rock-concert ticket, he wouldn't sleep through it, so why sleep through classes? He admitted that most class hours were not as exciting as a rock concert, but when he thought of class hours at $15 each, he attended regularly—and worked harder to prepare.

Malcolm and every other student knows that most learning does not take place in class. Class is where learning is guided, directed, tested, and measured. Tuition is paid largely for that direction, that impetus, yes, even that inspiration. But long hours of study outside the classroom are essential.

The high school relationships to leave behind are mostly romantic ones. About half of high school graduates are romantically involved. Half of that half may find their romantic attachment permanent. They may continue to love and finally marry their hometown honeys. Few of that group, however, leave their hometown either to work or to go to college. It is not easy to maintain a hometown romance if you're elsewhere, but there is indeed a sense of security in knowing someone is waiting back home. The hometown honey is a kind of insurance policy. If the whole business of college blows up in your face, at least there's someone back home who cares.

When Alice left for college, she made a deal with Arlen. "You go out with people here," she said, "and I'll go out with people at college. We'll test our love and see if it lasts. We'll talk about it at Christmas, OK?" Alice and Arlen made it through the first Christmas, but that was before Alice met Nate. The test continued.

The other difficult relationship to leave behind is the old childhood relationship with parents. This is one you may not be able to handle all by yourself. If your parents insist on babying you and keeping you tied to the apron strings—or purse strings—it will be difficult and embarrassing.

The first year my wife and I owned a farmhouse, we rented it to six college boys. It hadn't been lived in for two years, and it was quite a mess. Bob worked as hard as the rest of us to fix it up that fall. Unfortunately, Bob's mother showed up unexpectedly, and when she saw the house, she refused to let her son live there. Bob was embarrassed, but he couldn't go against his mother. She was paying the bills. He missed out on an interesting year of busy college activity mixed with serene country living. The other boys loved it.

College is a time for pulling up roots, for leaving home, for making many independent decisions. Many young men and women this age leave home for jobs or military training. They become instantly independent. They live elsewhere, earn their own money, and depend on their parents for nothing but love, prayers, and goodwill.

A college student, however, is economically tied to home. Students who earn enough to pay their own way and preserve their economic freedom are rare. Most can't survive without their parents' help. Parents know this, and some drive a hard bargain with their cold cash, keeping Junior and Sis as dependent as possible, making them ask for and account for, not only every penny, but also every hour they spend. This is unfair. Such parents deny their kids the opportunity to mature, and they invite rebellion.

It's important for parents and student to establish a clear sense of economic responsibility beforehand. The student should have all the funds the family can spare consistent with her or his needs, but that money, once given, should be the student's, with only reasonable strings attached.

Ernie's dad wrote out the following list of rules when he gave him money for his first year at college:

Don't buy a car, stereo, ski equipment, etc.

Your college money is a loan. Interest of six percent will begin the day you graduate. We'll work out a repayment schedule when you get your first job.

Budget your money and your time. Come home for Christmas, but not in debt.

If your parents tend to hover over you, you might be wise to choose a college far enough away from home to keep their visits to a minimum.

Show them, when they do visit, that you have things under control: room cleaned, clothes arranged, books and papers in order. Discuss ideas rather than things. Work at having some of your monthly allowance left over.

Your parents do have a right to expect you to try to be responsible. If you spend all your cafeteria money on pizza and cassette tapes, they may say you can jolly well starve for 10 days until your next check is due. As you learn to accept the consequences of your decisions, you will gradually be able to prove to your parents that you can live like an adult, live alone, live within your means, live morally and sensibly. If you do that, your parents may just leave you alone to do more of the same.

WHAT SHOULD I STUDY ?

"Try new things," Pastor Anderson had said. As Mary thought about college courses, verses and phrases began to run through her head: "Better things for better living." CHEMISTRY. "The earth is the Lord's and the fulness thereof." BIOLOGY. "If I had a fulcrum, I could move the earth." PHYSICS. "In the beginning was the Word." LIT-ERATURE. "Seek ye first the kingdom of God" (KJV). RELIGION. "Whenever the evil spirit . . . was upon Saul, David took the lyre and played it." MUSIC.

When you try to choose what to study in college, you may feel like a kid in an old-fashioned candy store. There are so many possibilities that you may wish you were two or three people so you could take more courses. The catalog, even at a small college, lists dozens of tantalizing and invit-ing courses of study. As college freshmen, most of us follow our high school interests and try to capitalize on our strengths.

George Turner took mostly math and chemistry and physics elective courses for his first two years of college, because he had done well in those subjects in high school. Then he began hanging around the art studio with Nancy, and he discovered that he had both an interest in and aptitude for art. He changed his major from science to fine arts. It is two years now since he graduated. He is happily though barely supporting himself with a small pottery studio.

As we enroll for our first courses, most of us are concerned about whether we can make the grade in college. We tend to choose those subjects that were easiest for us in high school. This works well for many students. Good musicians in high school can register for extra music courses and become even better musicians in college. They should learn, though, that music isn't everything, either in college or in life.

Some teachers have ways of pointing out and helping us polish our hidden talents. The wise student will listen to them and try what they suggest.

Jean Gleason was an outstanding basketball player in high school. She started college as a physical education major. In her freshman English class, she was surprised that Professor Frear thought she wrote well. Jean began to take writing seriously, and her interest in words led to an interest in literature. She changed her major, and now she's teaching high school English, coaching the basketball team, and occasionally publishing a poem.

Most of us have multiple interests and aptitudes. High school doesn't awaken them all. Some will surface in college; some will appear even later in life. Because we cannot predict all our interests or know what vocational opportunities we may have in years to come, we can best prepare if we take advantage of the wide variety of courses and try new things.

Matina Horner, president of Radcliffe College, told columnist Ellen Goodman, "I don't think people are going to have one-track careers anymore. Society can't absorb it. There's going to be more career shifting, second careers, third careers." This prediction is terribly important for those entering college. If you're not likely to work at one career until you retire, then you'd better prepare for two or three.

But how do you prepare for several careers? It isn't as hard as it sounds. A hobby may in time become a vocation.

LaVerne Remme was a full-time church worker who farmed as a hobby. Over the years he bought 40 acres here, 80 acres there. He finally gave up his church job to become a full-time farmer. He wishes now that he had taken a course or two in biology or botany when he was in college.

When Malcolm Page registered for his first set of courses, his advisor, Professor Hall, suggested that he consider his hidden interests, hobbies, and avocations. "An unusual course might lead to something later," she said. Malcolm considered courses in filmmaking, astronomy, and geography. He decided on astronomy.

"But what if I fail astronomy?" Malcolm asked.

"Well, what if you do?" Professor Hall answered. "We allow some courses to be taken on a pass-fail basis, but even if you choose to register for a grade, you aren't likely to fail. The worst that can happen is that you might get a lower grade than usual. You can live with a C or even a D here and there on your transcript."

"But what if I want to go to graduate school?" Malcolm asked.

"When I went to graduate school to study writing, my tutor had a copy of my college transcript on his desk when I first met him. Before I could even express my concern about the couple of Ds on my record, he said with a smile, 'You did poorly in just the right things for a writer.' "

Smorgasbording courses is a great way to go. Some variety is built in to course requirements at liberal arts schools, but most students should experiment beyond that. In many university programs and most professional schools, students have to design in their own variety. Wherever you go to school, give yourself a taste of as many different fields and disciplines as you can. You owe it to yourself—and to those three or four vocations you may pursue later in life.

Her college advisors will tell Mary Laurence that she shouldn't worry if her studies don't seem to be leading to any clear vocational goal. Mary, like most college students, is in what Gail Sheehy calls the Pulling Up Roots period in college. "Most of us during this period of exploration are vague if not void of ideas about what we should do. We generally begin by defining what we *don't* want to do" *(Passages,* p. 90). The beauty of not having definite vocational goals is that we are encouraged to sample. Once we have eliminated what we absolutely don't want, we can explore what we do want.

In exploring our interests, we sometimes forget what a rich cultural center a campus is. In any given week or month, there are concerts, plays, lectures, readings, recitals, and performances that can broaden our interests, whet our appetites, and generally make us more knowledgeable about our world.

As we broaden our cultural and educational horizons, God expects us to mature spiritually, too. Every college and university town has rich opportunities for Christian students. In addition to religion courses, church colleges have Sunday morning worship, midweek services, and Bible-study groups right on campus. Volunteer teams also work with churches, retirement homes, and retarded children, and do other kinds of service. Universities have Christian student centers representing many denominations, some with resident pastors and lay workers who devote all their time to students. College years are a perfect time to inquire into other faiths, to visit other churches.

When Joe Dolan went to the university, he missed his local congregation. He attended services at the student center at first, but it didn't suit him somehow. He mentioned this to Pastor Anderson, who made a phone call to a pastor friend whose church was near the university. The very next week the youth pastor of that church came to Joe's dormitory room at 11:00 p.m. He and Joe talked until after midnight.

Now Joe attends church in town. His new congregation reminds him of his hometown congregation, and he's more comfortable. He's also meeting quite a few other university students there.

God doesn't quit loving us as we leave home for college or university. On the contrary, he cares for us all the more, knowing that when we leave home, make new friends, and form new social patterns, we will feel alone and afraid sometimes, and be sorely tempted sometimes, too. When you ask, "What should I study?" remember that God wants you to grow not only intellectually, but also spiritually. After all, what does it profit us if we gain the whole world of knowledge, but lose our own souls?

7

FRIENDS: DO I NEED THEM ?

Solitary confinement has always been the most severe kind of imprisonment, worse than torture, really. It was used very effectively as a brainwashing technique during the Korean war. It is also a radical type of psychotherapy used on extremely disturbed children.

Strangely enough, some otherwise normal young people put themselves into solitary. They shy away from adults and other teenagers alike. Their loneliness and isolation gradually have a crippling effect on them, and reentry becomes more and more difficult.

Plenty of Christian teenagers go through this kind of social upheaval toward the end of high school or during their college or early working years. They become involved in a lonely search for a future. Many are impatient and afraid as they search for God's plan for their lives. As that plan unfolds, they gradually discover who they are and where they are going and what kinds of people they want to be with—and have to be with—along the way.

While God's plan develops, they grope around, trying one group and another, one friend and another, one sweetheart and another. They accept and reject both individuals and groups. Some even reject their own families. They discover that who they are is somehow connected with who their friends are, who they choose to be with, and why. It is a lonely and confusing time, and no earthly cure seems to help.

When Kathy Benton quit her job at Antron Corporation to go back to college, she was highly motivated. She wanted to be a biologist so much that she tried to give up everything, even her friends, to achieve that goal. She used to spend time with both Mary Laurence and John Mulligan in high school, but now, even though they were in the same college, Kathy had no time for them.

"Have you seen anything of Kathy?" Mary asked John one day outside the science building.

"Not since freshman week. She works upstairs here," John answered, pointing up toward the biology labs. It hurt him to think of Kathy alone and working so hard. He remembered a party last Thanksgiving when they had been very close.

"I was really looking forward to spending some time with her," Mary said. "We had some good times together back in Forestburg."

"I know what you mean. I called her a few times for movies, concerts, just something to do together. . . ."

"And she said no?"

"Not exactly, only that she had to study. I never

46

see her anywhere, not even the cafeteria. Does she eat?"

"Everybody eats," Mary laughed. "Sounds like it's eating you to get turned down."

"I guess it is a little. How about *you* going with me to the game—then maybe a pizza afterwards?"

"OK, but only if we go halves on the pizza. Should I see if Kathy wants to go along?"

"Don't bother," said John, with resignation.

As he walked back toward the dormitory, John thought about his two years in the marines. That was a lonely time too. Being a Christian wasn't so easy when most of the guys thought fun was drinking and shacking up. Wherever he was stationed, though, he found a couple of good friends. That really helped in Germany when they were all so far away from home. They did a lot of walking, saw plenty of sights, and knew where the good food was in five different towns. If it hadn't been for his friends, John wasn't sure he could have stuck it out. He wondered if Kathy could keep going without friends. He didn't think so. Not for very long anyway.

John remembered when his family first moved to Forestburg. He was a sophomore and school had already started at Central High. He didn't know anybody. The kids seemed like snobs. They all had their cliques. He ate his lunch in the boys' restroom the first week rather than sit alone.

When he became friends with Scott Elstad later in the year, John told him about it. Scott couldn't believe it. He laughed at first and then got a funny-sad-concerned look on his face. "You ate in the *john?*" Then he laughed again. Scott had

never been alone or without friends. It would never occur to him to cut himself off, to isolate himself like Kathy was doing. He knew he needed people. Kathy would soon learn that, too.

Barbra Streisand used to sing, "People who need people are the luckiest people in the world." The truth is, they are the *only* people in the world. Those who say, "I don't need anyone; I can do it myself," are defying God, fooling themselves, and asking for sad times.

The middle and late teen years are a difficult and lonely time. Gail Sheehy says the late teens make you feel as if you have "flu of the personality." What we want above all in these years is to make friends, but we don't know quite how—and we are afraid. We want to be close to people, but we fear opening ourselves up. In his essay "Surrender as a Noble Course," Andrew M. Greeley says:

> The trouble with intimacy is that it means vulnerability. Everyone wants intimacy but few of us are very good at vulnerability. We pay lip service to "openness" and "trust," but usually these are mask words which we use to hide ourselves and keep others at bay. Get too close to me and I'll beat you over the head with my openness and trust.

Getting close to people is scary at any age. We unhitch only as much trust and confidence as experience tells us a given person can take, or that we can take in return. It takes a long time to find someone we can trust with our real selves, someone we can really spill our insides to and not drive him or her away. Such people may be professionals such as Pastor Anderson, or peers who become so important to us that we marry them or make them our lifelong friends.

In *The Chosen,* his earliest and most interesting novel, Chaim Potok has one of his father figures say to his son:

> "The Talmud says that a person should do two things for himself. One is to acquire a teacher. Do you remember the other?"
> "Choose a friend," I said.

49

Loneliness is the most devastating of human pains. Friends are so very important to us because they are a hedge against the pain of loneliness. John learned that in the marines. He will discover that close friends become even more important in later years as he hedges against death, the ultimate loneliness and separation.

Our earliest friendships usually depend on where we live, on who our parents spend time with, and on common activities. When we were little we played with next-door neighbors, our cousins, and maybe one or two of the kids in the scout pack .

By the time we're in high school, our families probably have little control over our friendships. We may not even like our cousins anymore— although bloodlines often draw people back to family friends in later years. Many high school kids choose friends for selfish reasons. We may choose to be with people who are good to be seen with, who are from the most popular group—or we would if we could.

The tragedy of snobby high school friendships is that in later years we discover some wonderful classmates we never really noticed or had time for years ago. We ask ourselves how we could have been so blind to such interesting people, such potentially good friends. Fortunately, even among relationships selfishly formed, there may be one or two friendships that will last a lifetime.

As your own life moves from high school to the next stage, you will discover that you need fewer friends, but they will be closer friends. In high school most kids have a dozen or more friends, kind of a gang they run around with. There may be only one or two of them with whom they would share their deepest secrets. As they grow older, that small inner circle of friends will be enough. Jesus dealt with thousands of people, but he did the special things in his ministry with only Peter, James, and John.

Most of us who are blessed with happy marriages also discover we have become friends with our spouses. To begin with, my wife was the mysterious object of a powerful set of feelings I called love. She is still something of a mystery, and the so-called love is a much broader set of feelings than at first, but what has really changed is that we have become friends. She is my first choice as a partner in almost any activity, and I do those activities she doesn't enjoy with less relish and perhaps less often because we don't share them.

As you move into young adulthood, you will probably notice that the age range among your friends will expand. Most high school kids choose friends within a year or two of their own age, but later they develop relationships with older and younger people. Although my wife and I are both in our 40s, we spend time wtih couples that range from newlyweds in their early 20s to a retired couple in their late 70s. We do different kinds of things with them, of course, but they help us understand who we were and who we are going to become.

If you get to know people of different ages and from different backgrounds, cultures, and economic levels, you can learn things about yourself and about friendships and marriages. And speaking of marriage, there is nothing more deadly to real friendships, especially in the late teen years, than the "everyone is a potential marriage partner" outlook. Sure, you may soon be ready for marriage—but the search for many friends should be going on alongside your search for one mate. Noel Cameron Gardner says:

> When marriage is the priority, every relationship is viewed through matrimonyscopes—marriage-tinted glasses. Even casual acquaintances are classified as potentials or non-potentials. Friendships become loaded with expectations that bleed them of their spontaneity and natural enjoyment. When all the marbles are played into the marriage bag (and one is playing for keeps), there is great pressure in the playing of every shot ("Ministering to the Unmarried," *Ministry,* Sept. 1978, p. 5).

Playing every shot is a tense business. It puts demands on potential friends that they ought not be asked to meet—and it also puts demands on you. The strange thing is that you probably think you can be yourself with ordinary friends, but that you have to be your "super self" with boyfriends or girlfriends. The person you finally marry will actually like you best when you are yourself —no sham, no pretense, no elevator shoes, no makeup—just yourself. Being yourself with someone you love is a pleasant relief. It will help make your home a comfortable place to strip off the masks you show to the outside world.

Making friends away from home is sometimes difficult. You may have been plenty lonely sometimes right in your own hometown, but that's nothing compared to the loneliness you're apt to feel when you leave home for college, your first job, military service, or marriage. The dormitory, the apartment, the barracks are not really home away from home; that's propaganda. Away from home you will feel a special need for friends. Where can you find them? Where are they hiding?

One of the best ways to make new friends and meet new people in a strange town is to join a church and become active in it. That's what happened to Joe Dolan at the university. He and his new friends were soon teaching Sunday school, helping with the youth group, or singing in the choir. Many of them attended Bible study and the young adult group, too. There are friends to be found in church.

Another way to meet new people is to affiliate with interest groups around town—the arts guild, the summer band, the ski club, Weight Watchers. In such groups you'll meet people with similar interests or problems, people with whom to share a concert or a ski weekend or a salad.

Finally, if you want to gain a friend, be one. The fruits of the Spirit are useful in making friends: love, joy, patience, kindness, goodness, faithfulness, gentleness, self-control (Gal. 5:22). How could anyone resist a friend with such qualities? If friends don't appear quickly enough, it's not because your teeth are crooked or your hair isn't blond, or you are too tall or short. It's more likely that the Spirit hasn't quite hung enough fruits on you yet. Go back to praying again, and trying again.

John Mulligan is learning more about being a friend in college. He was a bit hurt by Kathy's rejection of his friendship, but he cares about her and will try again. Perhaps he will understand her better next time and be a bit more gentle. Making friends is making ourselves available, vulnerable, opening ourselves to others.

> The vulnerable person is strong enough to risk getting hurt. . . .He can give himself to another human being not like a dive bomber crashing into an aircraft carrier or like a Mack truck crumpling a Volkswagen, but rather in a gentle and subtle process by which the other is invited, indeed seduced, to giving himself in return (Greeley, *Essays,* p. 288).

God gave himself to us in exactly this way in the miracle of Christmas. An advertising agent would call Christmas the soft sell. How quietly and subtly Jesus came into our world, into our lives, as a baby in a manger and later as a gentle man. We can learn lessons from him.

WHAT ABOUT SEX ?

At St. Andrew's College, Mary Laurence roomed with another freshman girl who lasted only six days. She was homesick and left school even before classes started. Mary was lonely, too, but not *that* lonely.

Anyone who leaves home will be somewhat lonely and homesick. Gail Sheehy says that "loneliness is the most common companion during one's first year . . . in college, a job, or the army."

One way to handle loneliness is to maintain fairly close contact with home at first. Phone calls, letters, and weekend visits are common in those first months away from home, although they are apt to dwindle to the occasional contact and the emergency request for money after the first year.

A second solution for loneliness is to adopt a foster family. If you look around, you may find someone who responds to you like a sister or brother. You can cultivate that friendship. When Mary and John are able to look back on their college years, they will discover that they became like sister and brother.

It is also wise to look for adults at your school or on the job who can act as foster parents. You may discover that the custodian in your dorm or the man painting in your office or a cook at the corner cafe has a daughter or son your age and will offer some good advice when you're confused or lonely.

Malcolm Page tried this during his first year at St. Andrews, but it backfired. He began to go regularly to Ms. Vogel's office for extra help with his freshman English essays. She was young and engaging. Malcolm fell for her. Fortunately, she recognized the signs, and they talked about it. Malcolm was more embarrassed than hurt. Most teachers can be personable and helpful while remaining very professional. Next time Malcolm will probably choose someone older.

It is usually in the peer group, though, that loneliness and the search for companionship and romance can lead to sexual exploitation. The social life, dating, and romance away from home contain plenty of risks. I interviewed a number of students last year, trying to compare attitudes toward promiscuity, abortion, and sex. What shocked me was what I discovered about abortion.

The annual abortion rate on the average small college campus, as near as I could discover from student and medical sources, was about one abortion for every 15 young women. One dorm counselor on a church-college campus told me that of 15 freshmen in her corridor, two had abortions before April. The problem is probably at least as serious for young working women, but statistics are harder to get. Apparently many young men and women are sexually active but haven't given it much thought. Such pregnancies don't often occur among people who have reasoned through these decisions.

Once young people start a pattern of rather casual social sex, even if they are knowledgeable and avoid pregnancy, there are still problems. A set of guilty and grubby feelings may develop that could eventually sour all their later sexual experiences. Ray Short describes this in his frank and sensible little book, *Sex, Love, or Infatuation: How Can I Really Know?*

> Each time you have sex . . . you feel guilt and fear and loss of self-respect. Over and over again this happens. You have sex, you feel fear and guilt and remorse. In time all of these negative feelings become associated with the sex act itself.

The result is that later, even in marriage, sex may continue to bring guilt and fear and remorse when it might be a blessing and a delight.

Kathy Benton met Paul Kedroski at Antron. They were both lonely away from home. They dated for weeks and became more and more physical in their expressions of affection. On the Monday before Thanksgiving, Paul hinted that Kathy should give up her apartment and move in with him.

While she was home for the holidays, Kathy spent an evening with some of her old friends. She and John Mulligan started talking, and soon she was telling him all about Paul and his offer.

"I really enjoy being with him. We seem right

together. Why shouldn't we live together?" Kathy asked in an unconvincing voice.

"Maybe you'll regret it later," John said.

"What is liberation if it isn't the right to decide for myself?"

When John dropped Kathy off at home, she still wasn't sure whether she should move in with Paul or not. John was sure, though—sure that she shouldn't. That night and many nights afterward he prayed hard for Kathy.

John wouldn't know it for more than two years, but Kathy decided that liberation also means the right to reject the so-called new morality, the right to postpone sex until marriage. Neither Kathy nor anyone else need feel any obligation to the new morality, to the money a guy may have spent on her, or to decisions about sex that she may have made in the past. She need not sell out to any philosophy or to any person at any price.

John Mulligan could have told Kathy that many men are uncomfortable with sexual pressures, too. They're ill at ease with their stereotyped roles as aggressors and playmakers. I was. When I got married at age 25, I was a virgin. Like John, I was a member of a silent majority. Snowed by a few big talkers, I was reluctant to admit to my friends that I had no sexual experience at all. I was silently proud, though, and looking back I am more thankful than proud, thankful that those difficult adolescent and young adult relationships were not made any more complicated by premarital sex.

Some of the people who knew me then might say, "Well, he was too shy, or too dumb." Maybe so, but there is always opportunity. We frequently

have a chance to say yes; we also have the right, maybe under God the obligation, to say no. It is much easier on everyone if the young man becomes the controlling influence, the one who stops the crescendo of a growing physical relationship.

Looking back, I don't feel deprived, and you won't either if you wait. I don't think I missed out on anything I couldn't make up for later. I don't think I was particularly frustrated or backward or unfulfilled. My wife didn't think I was too awkward or inexperienced to keep. In retrospect, it seems that the frustrated ones, the mixed-up ones, those least sure of their masculinity, were the sex machines who had to have a different girl every week. Some of the guys I knew who were like that in college still haven't straightened out their sex lives after 25 years.

Everybody knows that the social and moral climate in our society runs in cycles. The Gay '90s and the Roaring '20s were both followed by more conservative times and by the austerity of world wars. There hasn't been a world war to cap off the Sexy '60s or the Swinging '70s—but we seem to be on our way to more conservative times. We have, as the old Broadway song says, "gone about as fur as we can go."

Our generation is realizing that it has swallowed more than enough garbage about the new morality from Hollywood, Madison Avenue, and the Pauls of the world who have perfected a line of sociological lingo and offer to share their apartment and their moral swampland with any Kathy who will. Paul does not represent a new morality. The *real* new morality didn't appear in our generation. It appeared almost 2000 years ago when a doomed man in sandals said to his dozen followers, "A new commandment I give to you, that you love one another."

The 20th-century new morality has been saying, "Make love to one another." Jesus' first-century new morality says simply, "Love one another." There is a world of difference. With the unselfish love of Jesus, we should care at least as much about others as we do about ourselves. Fornication is almost always selfish, with concern for one's own pleasure outweighing concern for the other's good. If you don't believe it, just ask some Kathy who said yes and has discovered she is pregnant—and her Paul isn't around anymore.

Today's young Christians are becoming more and more aware that they are only stewards of their bodies. Christ's ownership of our bodies motivates us to take care of them, not only in how we use sex, but also with exercise and good nutrition.

But Christian wholeness in the teen years is most threatened by overemphasis of sex. Sex can become an idol that twists and distorts every thought and pushes Christ right out of our lives. When intercourse becomes as ordinary as a handshake or a good-night kiss, then sex has lost its mystery, its uniting power, and its God-given function as a beautiful and special blessing.

We are entering a new age. The pendulum has already begun to swing toward more concern for one another's reputations, self-respect, and moral training; toward a more careful weighing of the long-term consequences of one's acts; and toward a more mature analysis of what masculinity and femininity mean.

MARRIAGE: NOW OR NEVER ?

When Mary Laurence first went to talk with Pastor Anderson about her future, she thought she was quite close to marriage. Actually it would be more than seven years until she walked up the aisle, and it wasn't going to be Jerry there waiting for her.

From the time of our first crushes, our first dates, our first romances, most of us dream of what it would be like to be married. It's OK to dream of a special someone to share a life with, but it pays to look at those dreams, to learn beforehand what to expect from marriage, what it can do—and especially what it cannot do.

Marriage is infused with great hope. We expect more from marriage than from any other institution, probably because it is God's arrangement. Because God's promises are built into marriage, we expect great things, sometimes more than marriage can deliver.

We enter other important stages with less enthusiasm. When we start high school, we say, "ho hum"; when we take a job, we say, "well, maybe"; even when we become adult members of the church, we are apt to say only, "I hope." But when we get married, it's "Definitely, of course, yes, yes, yes!"

School and church are just hopeful maybes because we know people in school and church who *are* only hopeful maybes. But honestly now, haven't we all seen and known plenty of maybes in marriage, too? Maybe our own parents haven't worked it out all that well. "But," you say, "when *I* get married it's going to be different. We love each other. We won't even consider failure."

A positive attitude is good indeed. Nobody should get married thinking it isn't going to work. We all believe it's going to work, and work well. When we go to a wedding, even those who are widowed or divorced go with joy, with prayers for the young couple's happiness, expecting they will be happy. Those of us who have been married awhile know many frightening, negative things these newlyweds don't yet know, but we still have high hopes for them, maybe higher than the realities of our own married lives have proved possible. In *Bed and Board,* Robert F. Capon says:

> Marriage is a paradox second only to life itself. That at the age of twenty or so, with little knowledge of each other and a *dangerous overdose of self-confidence,* two human beings should undertake to commit themselves for life—and that church and state should receive their vows with a straight face—all this is absurd indeed.

I added the italics to Father Capon's quotation for emphasis. That "dangerous overdose of self-confidence" should concern Mary and Jerry and every other pair of young dreamers. You've heard the phrase, "Love conquers all"? Well, it doesn't. Love is not a conquerer.

I can't stress this enough. I wish this section could be in red ink so it would really catch the eyes of those of you who will marry in the next few years. The important truth is this: *Love and marriage will not conquer any of your demons.* If you are jealous now, you will probably be worse when you are married. If you are given to rage, you will probably still rage. If you are insecure, afraid, disturbed, or selfish, marriage is not likely to cure you.

You can't run away from home by getting married, either. Sure, home life can become intolerable for kids who don't communicate well with their parents. Put that together with the hopes and dreams that we all drape over marriage, and what does a young man or woman think? "I'll get married and get away from all this mess." Unfortunately, the getaway marriage never works.

Marriage succeeds when it is undertaken for positive reasons and when the decision to marry is mutual. I was becoming who God wanted me to be independently until I married. After I married, God had plans for *us.* Even God almighty can't merge two sets of plans, though, without some adjustments. Anne Morrow Lindbergh, widow of the famous aviator, says this is especially true of married women:

> With a new awareness, both painful and humorous, I begin to understand why the saints were rarely married women. I am convinced it has

65

nothing inherently to do, as I once supposed, with chastity or children. It has to do primarily with distractions. The bearing, rearing, feeding, and educating of children, the running of a house with its thousand details; human relationships with their myriad pulls—woman's normal occupations in general run counter to creative life, or contemplative life, or saintly life *(Gift from the Sea,* p. 29).

What she says may be true. Marriage does take time and makes demands on us, male and female alike. But simply being married is never the last experience God plans for us. Arliss Burton still looks dreamily at her wedding pictures. After 30 years she still thinks that was her big day. Someone should have told her years ago that marriage is not an end in itself. Sure, it is a way of living that achieves some ends, some goals—sexual, social, and financial—but it makes other goals more difficult.

Elizabeth Andreasson, a writer, translator, and homemaker, has been married 40 years. She has helped her husband professionally and reared six children to mature adulthood. Self-disciplined enough to work at her own projects early in the morning and late at light, she pleased both her husband and herself with her accomplishments —and probably God, too. Pursuing her goals within marriage was difficult, but not impossible.

My wife Judy has adopted a fairly useful philosophy in pursuing her professional career within marriage. She is a graphic artist. She has followed me around to churches and colleges all these years and done her wifely and motherly duty as she was able. Meanwhile, she did her artwork for whomever asked her. I sometimes complained in those early days about the meager pay she received. She never complained. She just kept designing brochures for churches, posters for colleges, letterheads for businesses. She got experience with both design and printers' techniques. When we finally settled down a few years ago and the kids became more independent, she had some experience and some samples of her work, and she was ready to get more deeply involved in her profession.

A young woman who wants to be both a homemaker and a career woman ought to promise herself right at the altar that she will do as much as she is able to do professionally within marriage. Developing her knowledge and skills will give her satisfaction, even if she chooses not to work full time outside the home. She will keep herself up-to-date professionally. Knowing she can work if she has to acts as an insurance policy against the loss of her husband.

Hobbies, too, are important—for men as well as women. Getting really good at anything is exciting and satisfying. If your hobby is growing roses, grow the best roses in the state. Find time now and plan to find time even in the busy early years of marriage to do some of the things you enjoy or have wanted to try. Many hobbies develop into vocations and become means of making or supplementing an income.

Tom Richards, a full-time air traffic controller during the day, relaxed at home by molding and firing ceramic candleholders for a small candle factory. The company that bought his holders was continually expanding, and Tom's work expanded with it. He now works part time at the control tower and full time at his basement business. He and his wife work together on the ceramics. Their marriage has been enriched, and they are both home more with their children.

Marriage should devour no one. It can and must be kept in perspective. If marriage is a part of your plan, God will expect you to learn all you can about marriage, to talk about it with friends, relatives, your pastor. It's never too late, either, to ask your parents how marriage has helped or hindered their development as persons, how they have seen their plan, God's plan, and their marriage working together, or pulling them in several directions.

Although it may be difficult, you should probably try to discover whether marriage is really what you want—now, or sometime, or ever. Surely not everyone should get married. If you're not sure, it certainly can't hurt to wait. People are marrying later; some are choosing not to marry at all. Anthropologist Margaret Mead observed in "From Popping the Pill to Popping the Question" that our society no longer expects or demands that everyone be married.

> The family is not dead. It is going through stormy times, and millions of children are paying the penalty of current disorganization, experimentation, and discontent. In the process, the adults who should never marry are sorting themselves out. Marriage and parenthood are being viewed as a vocation rather than as the duty of every human being (Essays, p. 131).

The church takes seriously the challenges and

responsibilities of marriage and urges us to be responsible husbands, wives, and parents. Recently the church has begun to consider dual roles, dual responsibilities, the sharing of both earning and homemaking. God's plan for your life can be both beautiful and useful, whether you marry or not. But if you do marry, his plan for you need not drop into any predetermined ruts the minute you say, "I do."

CAN I LIVE WITH STRANGERS ?

When Kathy Benton took a job in the city, she left Forestburg to share an apartment with two other young women. When John Mulligan went into the marines, he traded his cozy room for a barracks. When Mary, Scott, and Mark, chose St. Andrews College, they moved into dormitories.

As vocational decisions change our lives, they often change our living arrangements. We have all made changes before. To begin with, we were all very comfortably housed in our mothers' wombs. Food, shelter, and warmth were automatic. When we popped out and began to cry, our parents had to make other arrangements. At first we probably slept in cribs in or near our parents' rooms. When we were older, and maybe other children came along, some of us shared a room. Others were afforded the luxury of their own rooms.

Your living arrangements will continue to change as your life unfolds. Some of the options you may have to face in the next few years are these:

1. The college dormitory
2. A private or shared apartment
3. Living with a family not your own
4. Living at home while you study or work
5. Newlywed housing

A college dormitory is a very specialized dwelling. It is designed to be convenient to classrooms and cafeteria, to be economical to build and maintain, and to provide reasonably priced sleep, relaxation, and study space for fairly large numbers of students.

When Mary Laurence went to St. Andrews, she was assigned a room in the freshman dorm. She wasn't sure what to expect. She had visited the campus during her senior year, and she thought all the dorm activities—the visiting from room to room, the laughing and horseplay, the popcorn parties—were all great fun. She read in the college catalog that the dormitory was like a home away from home, a place to study and sleep and relax. Mary looked forward to it.

What the catalog didn't say was that when 200 young people live in the same building, they all study and sleep and relax at different times. About the only things they do on a predictable schedule is go to class and eat.

Mary got into a routine of getting up very early, about 5 a.m. She would study for two hours, then jog a mile, then shower and go to breakfast. The schedule was tight for days she had 8:00 classes, just right for 9:00 days. The problem was Carrie. After Mary's first roommate went home, Carrie moved in. Carrie was a night person. She studied late and never ate breakfast. Mary and Carrie had adjustments to make.

If you live in a dorm, you will learn to make adjustments. The problem is to avoid disturbing others, being disturbed yourself, and getting angry. Anger is the worst of it. Avoiding anger may mean finding another place to study sometimes; it may mean locking yourself in your room; it may mean a nose-to-nose confrontation with your roommate as you try to juggle schedules. What you tell yourself as you get more and more tired and more and more irritated is that dorm living is part of the college experience, you are meeting lots of people, and it isn't forever. Vacations and breaks provide time for rest and recuperation. You will need

vacations for just that. Putting off the big term paper until Christmas break only means you won't get the rest you need.

Kathy Benton had a different experience in her city apartment. The two young women she found to live with her also worked regular hours. There was a bit of bathroom door banging in the mornings, but most days they all got home around 5:30, shared supper, then did a variety of things together or separately in the evenings.

As time went on, though, Kathy found that she had less and less in common with her apartment mates. Penny was a party person; Amy was shy and quiet. They both borrowed her things continually, often without asking. Sometimes on Saturday nights Kathy was expected to get lost until 1:00 so Penny could entertain Jack. On a couple of those nights Kathy felt like a skid-row person, wandering the city with no place to go. She never asked the others to get lost, even when she was dating Paul. She thought of getting an apartment of her own, but she knew that even if she could afford it, she would be lonely. All shared housing is a trade-off, she thought.

John Mulligan tried something different. During his freshman year most of the guys in the dorm seemed terribly young to him, but he stuck it out for the year. That spring he hunted around and found the Sherwins, a family with an upstairs room for rent. John and the Sherwins were perfect for each other. They treated him like their own son. Although he was expected to eat in the college cafeteria, he ate dozens of breakfasts with the Sherwins, and a few dinners, too. They kept on inviting him. He showed his appreciation by mowing the lawn, shoveling the walks, and generally helping out around the house. The Sherwins even kept John's parents overnight when they came for the spring concert. John felt like he had two sets of parents under the same roof.

John had friends, though, whose room rentals weren't so successful. The more they talked about it, the more they recognized the special dynamics in each family, and how those dynamics are affected by the addition of a nonfamily person into the home. In one of the families, loss of privacy was the big issue. Suddenly Dad couldn't run around in his underwear looking for a clean pair of socks; Sis couldn't parade through from the basement shower wrapped in a towel. The smells and sounds of human plumbing seemed embarrassing—especially at first. Even John felt that.

Where the living arrangements worked out best, people had learned to ask lots of questions: how spaces were to be used, whose car was going to be parked where, who got the bathroom and how long. It became crucial to communicate, to talk over the large and small details of shared family life.

If the student or wage earner lives at home, the situation is potentially explosive. When Alice Potter finished high school, she expected an added measure of freedom to come automatically. She thought her parents would start treating her like an adult. She planned on setting her own hours, having whatever guests she chose in her room whenever she chose, eating in or out whenever she wished.

Parents don't give up control so easily. Alice's didn't, and neither will yours. If you try living at home while going to college or working, you're going to have to expect control. Your parents may expect you to live pretty much as you always did. Since most parents maintain normal work-sleep schedules, it may be OK for you to have a friend over to study or talk until 3:00 a.m.; it may *not* be OK to keep your parents awake.

If you are a student living at home, everyone will agree that study is your main job and will adjust to that, but putting in your licks at the dishpan, the dustmop, and the lawnmower will keep you from becoming a china doll in your own home.

Likewise if you are working and living at home. A normal job leaves you plenty of hours to help out around the house—and it makes sense to do so. If you think you're too tired after work, consider what Dad often does around home after working all day. If Mom works outside the home, too, she certainly doesn't come home and flop on the couch for the evening. Everyone in a well-managed home needs to help.

Even though you have a job and earn your own money, you are still costing your parents quite a bit. Diane sat down with her mother one day to figure out just how much. There were five in the family, so they calculated one-fifth of the house payments, one-fifth of the utility bills, one-fifth of the groceries. That gave them a place to start working out a room-and-board payment plan. Ann Landers suggests 25% of your take-home pay. Whatever you decide, it should be reasonable and take into account that this is a family matter. Most families strike a figure somewhere near half what they would charge a nonfamily renter.

If your parents don't expect or want to be paid, you could suggest putting your "rent" into a scholarship fund for your kid brother; you might use an amount equivalent to rent to buy your parents useful household items or give them gift certificates; or you might give the extra money to your church or some charity. If you are earning a living, try to pay your own way. It's like St. Paul said in his second letter to Thessalonica, "If any one will not work, let him not eat" (3:10).

Even though St. Paul gives them permission, your parents love you too much to starve you out. You'll have to act responsibly on your own. Try to help with the work, pay your way, and keep your welcome warm.

If you marry, housing may be a problem. Rents may seem out of sight, and buying a house with a large down payment and large monthly payments will seem even worse. You may be tempted to move in with one or the other set of parents. They have plenty of space, maybe even a basement apartment or a mobile home in the backyard.

Beware. The Bible says to "leave father and mother" and be with your husband or wife. Living with family beyond a short stay is inviting dependence.

Brad and Althea moved into an abandoned farmhouse soon after their marriage. It was drafty and leaky, but they agreed to fix it up for the farmer as payment for rent. They learned to heat largely with wood, to grow much of their own food, and to live very simply and frugally. Living by themselves and beginning their married life with very few outside pressures, they're learning to be self-sufficient and independent.

Living with someone new is a challenge for most teenagers. Like all challenges, it is a learning, growing experience. Our Christian faith, that solid center of our lives, helps us immensely with these relationships, too. Christ's challenge, "Love your neighbor as yourself," applies to roommates, apartment mates, in-laws, everybody. You will be reminded again and again of the fruits of the Spirit, and you will be led to see the strangers you live with as brothers and sisters in the family of God.

HOW DO I FEEL ABOUT WORK ?

Any particular job can be wonderful or terrible, depending on the conditions. Take washing dishes, for instance. Washing dishes used to be a terrible chore at the Laurence house. Then they moved the TV next to the kitchen sink. Now the living room (where the TV used to be) stays neater, they watch less TV (because kitchen chairs are less comfortable), and whoever is at the dishpan is king or queen of the channel selector. When Mary is standing there doing dishes, she can say to her brother, "If you want to watch cartoons so bad, come here and finish these dishes." Then he must decide how important those cartoons really are.

Pastor Anderson often talks about the good times he's had at church camps washing dishes after supper. It was a high old time among the KP crew, throwing dishrags around, splashing soapsuds on each other as they turned a chore into fun.

How we feel about work depends on where we do it, with whom we do it, why we do it, and how it challenges our potential. The Bible has a lot to say about work. Jesus himself said many different and baffling things:

Do not labor for the food which perishes, but for the food which endures to eternal life (John 6:27).

It is like a man going on a journey, when he leaves home and puts his servants in charge, each with his work (Mark 13:34).

Do not be anxious about your life, what you shall eat or what you shall drink, nor about your body, what you shall put on (Matt. 6:25).

Consider also some of the parables: The two sons working in the vineyard (Matt. 21:28-31), the prodigal son and his brother (Luke 15:11-32), the workers in the vineyard (Matt. 20:1-16), the talents (Matt. 25:14-30). After we have read these and others, we aren't at all sure whether Jesus says to work hard and provide for ourselves or to take it easy and let God provide.

After Adam and Eve had sinned and were thrown out of the garden, part of the curse seemed to involve hard work: "In the sweat of your face you shall eat bread till you return to the ground" (Gen. 3:19).

At her father's funeral, Arliss Burton lamented over and over that he had to work so hard all through his life. Actually, her father loved hard work. Some of us really do. I thoroughly enjoy hard physical work, and the sense of accomplishment at the end of a hot, sweaty day. Many young people learn early to enjoy work—and some who hate work in their early years learn that working hard for a family they love, on homes or yards they enjoy, or at important or useful jobs is actually challenging and enjoyable.

We need to avoid extremes in our attitudes toward work. At one extreme are those who couldn't care less. This country has plenty of half-speed employees who aren't concerned about what kind of work they do or what the consequences of their sloppy or lazy attitudes will be. An employee leaves an assembly line to get a cup of coffee, neglecting to tighten one end of the steering arm on a car. As a result, a child ends up in a wheelchair the rest of his life.

In a recent survey of 18 nations, our amazing industrial U.S.A. ranked at the very bottom in productivity increase. Even easygoing Italy was ahead of us. Japan, at the top of the list, showed an increase eight times higher than ours.

There are many reasons for this, many factors involved, but too many Americans obviously are not taking pride in their work or working hard at their jobs. Perhaps many of them stay at jobs they don't like because they are afraid to change. For such people wages go up and up but productivity stays about the same.

No matter what you try to do, try to get really good at it. All good employees apply themselves to challenges, get the best training they can, and continue to learn on the job, as long as they have the job. But good workers can overdo it, too. Some people do indeed work too hard and take themselves and their jobs too seriously. Gail Sheehy has a description of such a person. She calls him a *wunderkind*—wonderboy. He is young, under 30,

and could be a businessman, farmer, preacher, anything:

> Work is what he thinks about. Work is his fix. The dividing line between work and private life is blurred early. He works at parties, in the shower, in his fitful early-waking dreams; he works even at play. The point of the vacation is to recharge his batteries for more work; the point of the golf game is to sew up a business friendship, unless the point of the same is even more basic: to win the championship *(Passages,* p. 272).

Scott Elstad enjoys a good relationship with his father. They spend a lot of time together—now. Scott can remember a few years, though, when all his father did was work. He was never around. Scott's mother seemed to resent the work then, too. Now Scott can look back at those years and see clearly that his father was in a *wunderkind* stage.

Unfortunately, a few people never get out of this stage. Jesus' parable of the foolish farmer (Luke 12:13-21) was about such a man. Bigger and bigger, more and more was his philosophy, even at the expense of his spiritual life and his soul.

People's work shouldn't drive them away from God. When it does, they obviously are not following God's plan for their lives. The problem is usually pride, that feeling that you can conquer the world by yourself.

Giants in the Earth is a great pioneer novel by Norwegian immigrant O. E. Rölvaag. Almost anyone who has prairie pioneer ancestors becomes engrossed in this classic story of the struggles of early settlers. The hero, Per Hansa (Peter Hanson), is a pioneer farmer on the Dakota prairies. He has come to the prairie with nothing, and he's making it big. Everything he does turns out right. He handles every crisis: dry weather and wet, locusts, Indians, Irish claim jumpers. His neighbors believe, and soon Per Hansa comes to believe, that he can do anything.

When a friend is dying, Per Hansa's wife insists that he go out in a Dakota blizzard to fetch a pastor. Per Hansa is concerned, but he straps on his skis and strikes out, believing he can make it. He does not. He freezes to death out on the prairie, a victim of his absolute belief in himself.

People who believe absolutely in themselves may not freeze to death like Per Hansa, but they will surely die—like the rich farmer: "Fool! This night your soul is required of you" (Luke 12:20).

Vocational decisions are different for young

Christians because they trust not only in themselves, but also in a forgiving, loving, guiding Savior. Sure, it's important to cultivate good feelings about work, but it is even more important to sense God's direction, sometimes even God's pressure in our choices of jobs and preparation for jobs. If there are two or more jobs, two or more options at a given time, the decision is never neutral. God sees one choice as better, another as worse.

As Christians we are constantly reminded that we are servants. The several jobs we may choose and work at through our lives may or may not be *directly* related to Christian service, but they should make us feel we contribute to the society in which we live; they should challenge our abilities; they should make us feel good about what we do; and they should provide opportunities for witness and service.

When Jean Gleason began coaching and teaching, she had opportunity after opportunity to witness to her teams and to share her counsel and her faith with a few students who were in deep trouble and with dozens of others who needed only an occasional nudge in the right direction. Helping people is what Jean really loves about her work. Helping people is what every Christian wants and needs. Helping people makes Christians young and old feel good about their work, about the paths along which God is leading them.

12

HOW DO I DECIDE WHAT TO DO ?

When he was home for Christmas, Malcolm took a quiz about work that was in the Sunday paper. He was surprised at how many kinds of work he had already done. He had cleaned and mowed and cooked and gardened; he had worked on cars and run machinery; he had painted, taught little kids in cub scouts, and baby-sat for the kid next door. The list seemed to go on and on. The article suggested that he had already worked at many jobs that were somebody's vocation, somebody's way of making a living. In limited ways, he had already been a chef, agronomist, mechanic, artist, and teacher.

The more Malcolm thought about the kinds of work he would like to do, the more confused he became. He'd been aware that the number of jobs to choose from had multiplied since his parents finished school, but then he read that well over half the jobs men and women now work at were absolutely unheard of 25 years ago.

Malcolm tried to pick a job by figuring out what he had an aptitude for. He took some aptitude tests from the school counselor. Then he began to page through lists of jobs in the counselor's dog-eared pamphlets, the same ones that dozens of other kids, just as confused, had already studied. The lists made his head swim. "There are too many jobs," he finally said. "I can't decide."

Malcolm could have focused his choices much better if he had been told that aptitude and need are two different things. If I went to a vocational counselor and took an aptitude test, he would probably tell me to look for work as an auto mechanic. He would be right; I have the aptitude. I built my own motorbike when I was 14, bought my first car (Model T Touring) when I was 15, and have been working on cars and motorcycles ever since. I understand and enjoy machinery. It is a challenge unlike my other work, and it gives me special satisfactions. I also enjoy saving money by doing my own repairs.

But I have other needs stronger than the need to fix cars. Like most kids I began to sort out those needs in high school, letting my needs help focus my aptitudes. As the years went by, I noticed that in addition to mechanical ability, I also had some aptitude for study, for teaching, and for preaching. Now I am a professor/preacher who fixes cars on the side. Had my needs been only slightly different, I might be an auto mechanic teaching in a vocational school, doing lay preaching on the side.

Everyone has a variety of aptitudes. As you gradually learn what God wants you to do, some of your aptitudes will rise above others; some will be major, some minor. A girl with a high aptitude for some sport may try to become a professional athlete. If that aptitude is slightly less strong than her business or teaching aptitude, she may end up managing a ski shop or coaching a golf team.

But even people with ideal jobs don't have all their needs answered by work, any more than their earlier needs were all answered by being a student. In *Reading,* Warren Boroson says:

> As Dr. Alan McLean, an IBM psychiatrist, points out, the healthiest people usually have various sources of satisfaction; they are lawyers, say, but they are also spouses, parents, friends, citizens, churchgoers, art lovers, stamp collectors, golfers, and so forth. If such people lose their jobs, or if their work becomes less satisfying or its quality starts deteriorating, they have not lost their sole interest in life, the only prop to their self-esteem.

Trying to find that just-right combination of job and hobbies and interests is one of the big challenges of Christian vocation. It is a matter of seeking balance. It's important to remember that today's choice isn't always tomorrow's choice.

After their third session, the counselor bet Malcolm a hamburger that if he went downtown on Thursday night when the stores were open, he couldn't find two out of 25 people over 40 who were still working at their first full-time jobs. Friday noon in the cafeteria, Malcolm treated the counselor to a hamburger.

Job mobility is a fact of modern life. Today's job choice is not likely to last forever. Opportunities arise, new interests surface, different jobs open up. Pressures not related to jobs force people to move, to change, to try something new.

It isn't this kind of change that spooks people, though; it is fear of change. Fear torpedoes more opportunities than either lack of ability or training. Christians contemplating changes, ready to make changes, should continually remind themselves that "all things work together for good to those who love God" (Rom. 8: 28 KJV), even the bad moves. The misery Mark may endure one year in one job may force him to seek out the much better situation he finds himself in the following year.

Our aims and goals change, too. When I was a senior in high school, I wanted to be a civil engineer—a surveyor. A year later I wanted to be a meteorologist. A year after that I wanted to be a physicist. I never became any of those things, and it hasn't really mattered. I have taken courses and made preparations for work I never did. That didn't matter much, either. I have also worked at jobs for which I *wasn't* prepared. That did matter.

If we let ourselves be urged or pressured into jobs for which we aren't prepared, we're asking for a lot of tension. Scott Elstad was friendly and popular and captain of the baseball team, but that didn't necessarily mean he would be a good student council president. A good teacher won't always make a good principal or dean. Being a good car salesman doesn't qualify someone to manage the agency.

On the other hand, every new job is scary. Many jobs include training during the early months and weeks, and employers expect mistakes at first. Making a wrong or ill-advised choice is never the bitter end. God can use any of our choices. The Bible is full of stories of wrongheaded people who were turned around in their tracks: Jonah, Isaiah, St. Paul.

Kathy Benton was only slightly distracted from her path during her short stay in the city and her job in a big corporation; in fact, that may have been God's path for her all along. She learned plenty about herself during those months and was far more ready to search out her more lasting pathways afterward.

Sometimes what we do is not as important as who we do it with. Many of us spend well over half our waking hours with coworkers. Working well together can make work satisfying and important. So as you consider a certain job or career, investigate a bit to find out how people in that kind of work relate to one another. You may save yourself later disappointments.

When Ms. Vogel began to train for teaching college English, the life of a college professor looked exceptionally good to her. She liked to think of having a flexible schedule, working with people, being respected. After she began teaching, though, she discovered that infighting and professional jealousy among the faculty made the job less enjoyable than she'd expected.

Investigating job possibilities and career options is largely a matter of being inquisitive, of not being satisfied with the pat answer, the easy way. Jim Burton has always wanted to take over his parents' farm, and maybe God wants him to do just that. But he is determined to prepare well first, with ag school and maybe liberal arts, too.

Mark Hanson was a farm boy, too, and everyone would have accepted his staying on the farm as the natural thing to do. But his dreams were elsewhere, and he looked elsewhere.

No one should be satisfied with the easy answer, which sometimes means doing what parents want. What they want for us may be right and may be what God wants, too—but we have to find that out for ourselves.

Chaim Potok, author of *The Chosen* and several other novels, has inspired and informed many readers. His mother wanted him to be a doctor and was greatly disappointed that he wanted to write. Although he might have become a very competent physician, it is fortunate for all his readers that he followed his own inclinations. He studied and worked and trained to be the best writer he could be. He has been rewarded for his efforts.

Trying to decide what to do is indeed a struggle, but struggle we must. The rewards of finding just the right work are great for anyone, but greatest for the Christian. Getting on with what we feel to be God's plan and intention is very satisfying and will ultimately result in lives more and more devoted to Christian service.

HOW DO I FIND A JOB ?

No job is unimportant. Here are stories about two relatives of mine who weren't too excited about their jobs as dishwashers the first week or two.

A nephew in Denver applied for a job at a restaurant. There was an opening for a dishwasher. It didn't seem like much, but he took it—and took it seriously. While he was doing the best job he could with the dishes, he watched how the waitresses, cook, and busboys did their jobs. Soon he was offering advice to new waitresses and busboys, helping them get started.

Now he travels for the restaurant chain. Wherever they open a new restaurant, he spends several weeks there training new staff. He moved from dishwashing to personnel management simply because he cared how people did their jobs. He now has a very portable skill, and some experience to go with it.

One of my cousin's boys took a job as a dishwasher in a pancake house after high school. He did his job well, and they liked him. When one of the cooks resigned, he asked for the job and got it. While flipping pancakes and frying bacon, he was surprised to discover in himself a real love for food preparation. He applied for and won an apprenticeship with a chef in Switzerland. He is now one of the chefs at a Minneapolis men's club.

No job is unimportant. Even if it doesn't lead to a promotion, the job itself is important. Ever had a sticky plate or a gooey fork in a restaurant? Bad dishwashing is bad for business. When a bad dishwasher hears of a different job he might like to try, where is he going to get a letter of recommendation? No job is unimportant.

In *The Art of Living Treasure Chest,* Wilfred A. Peterson says that making any job important is simply a matter of "making your work *you.*"

> It is putting the stamp of your unique personality on the work you do. It is pouring your spirit into your task. It is making your work a reflection of your faith, your integrity, your ideals.

Lucha Jerusal did exactly that. She was born in Mexico, one of 16 children. A Minnesota couple sponsored her immigration, and she worked for them as a housekeeper. She later got a custodial job at a hospital in Minneapolis. Columnist Robert T. Smith told about her in the *Minneapolis Tribune* (Sept. 18, 1978):

> The first thing she did was decorate her housekeeper cart. "Why not pretty?" she said. She put multicolored ribbons on it. With her bright cart and brighter smile she brought joy to hundreds of patients until her death.

Or take our milkman, Frank Haugen. He has been delivering milk in this area for 25 years. He loves it—it's useful work, and it allows him to go from house to house like a one-man good-cheer committee. He spends a minute here, five minutes there, with a funny story, some local history, a bit of philosophy. He is forever trading books and ideas with the many college professors on his route. He has put his own stamp on his work.

Or consider the garbage truck in Rochester, Minnesota, that has this sign painted gaily on its side:

IF YOU ARE NOT SATISFIED WITH
OUR SERVICE,
DOUBLE YOUR GARBAGE BACK.

In the same fleet is a truck with a row of dolls lined up on top of the cab. The driver has saved all the dolls he could find in the garbage. He not only uses them for cab ornaments, he gives many away to children on his route.

The problem is sometimes to find a job, any job, into which you can pour your spirit. There may be no jobs.

Vivian graduated from a church college last year with a degree in music education and a teaching certificate. There were no jobs available. Did she sit around and complain or apply for unemployment compensation? No. She went home to work on the farm. Right now she's milking 80 cows for a neighbor who injured his hand. She's also singing in church. Maybe she sings in the barn, too. Someday soon, some school system is going to get a terrific music teacher who can also manage a dairy operation.

When we enter the job market, most of us work at what we can, where we can, when we can. If we're smart, we do the best we can, even if it's washing dishes, because the better we do, the more we enjoy our work and the sooner something new will show up.

Apart from some hard-core situations that defy even the experts, most unemployment is simply a matter of saying that we won't work at *certain* jobs. There is always work to be done. Some jobs —like dish washing—go begging for lack of applicants.

While he looked for more agreeable work, Bill Burton told himself he would work at some job, any job, that gave him some free business hours for job hunting. He got a part-time job as a waiter and continued to interview for other jobs.

Once as he was about to leave the house for an interview, he looked in the mirror and asked himself, "Would I hire someone who dresses like I do, who wears his hair like I do, who comes on like I do?" His answer was yes—except that maybe he needed a haircut. He told himself that if he didn't get this job he would get a haircut before his next interview.

When you go looking for a job, any job—part-time, summer, or full-time—try to look and be at your best when you apply. Kirby Stanat worked as a job recruiter on college campuses for 13 years, and during that time hired about 8000 young people for business and industry. He says those who hire are tremendously influenced by appearances. In "Want a Job?" he describes a typical campus job interview from the time you, the applicant, enter the door:

> As you scrape past, he gives you a closeup inspection. He looks at your hair; if it's greasy, that will bother him. He looks at your collar; if it's dirty, that will bother him. He looks at your shoulders; if they're covered with dandruff, that will

bother him. If you're a man, he looks at your chin. If you didn't get a close shave, that will irritate him. If you're a woman, he checks your makeup. If it's too heavy, he won't like it *(Essays, p. 72)*.

And so on. Stanat said that by the time an applicant sits down to begin the interview, the recruiter's mind is 75% made up. First impressions count.

Another tip—don't get your mind set on only one type of job when you go in for an interview. My friend Arlen answered an ad for a quality-control job, and the personnel manager said the position was already filled. Before he walked out the door, Arlen asked a question every job applicant should ask before he leaves: "Do you have anything else available?" The manager said, "Only a liaison person for our plant in Norway—but the applicant would have to speak Norwegian." Arlen said, "I speak Norwegian." He turned around and sat down. Three weeks later he began flying back and forth between Chicago and Oslo.

When we need a job, we often forget the contacts and tips that can come from family and friends. Although laws now require that many jobs be advertised, many other jobs, perhaps most other jobs, are filled by word of mouth: "I'll tell my cousin about it," "My brother's looking for a job." Tell everyone you know you're job-hunting, and let them help you look. Use your contacts. Then, when you walk into the door for that interview, you can mention the name and have an immediate common ground: "My aunt Susan Willowby suggested I apply for the position you have open in. . . ." The person behind the desk may talk about Aunt Susan first, but the job interview will follow.

Bill Burton finally used a bit of influence to get his first job, but he knew that keeping it was his own worry. No amount of influence can keep a job. Bill knew he had to figure out what his employer expected of him as a fair return for his wages, and he tried to do that, plus a bit more. Bill remembered what Jesus said—if they ask you to walk a mile, walk two—and he tried always to give more than was required. It was that extra measure that made him a memorable employee and brought his name to mind when his supervisor was transferred. "Let's try Bill. He's young, but he always does a good job."

Beyond doing what was expected and a bit more, Bill found that the best advice for keeping a job was to take his Christian principles right along with him. He figured if he couldn't keep a job by following Christ's teachings, then the job probably wasn't worth keeping. He asked himself, "What worthwhile job could be lost by following such advice as 'love your enemy?' " (And he did acquire a few enemies, especially after he was promoted.)

Bill hung up a list of the fruits of the Spirit alongside his desk. The list reminded him of his challenge, it helped him discover other Christians in his department, and it inspired those who read it to try to be patient and kind.

14

WHAT IF I CHANGE MY MIND ?

Mary Laurence learned lots of things about herself while she was in college. She tried many different kinds of courses, sorted out options and needs and aptitudes, and finally chose a major in sociology. After she graduated she got a job with an educational testing service. She also married Scott Elstad—whom she couldn't stand in high school, by the way. When he was captain of the baseball team and president of the student council, she thought he was stuck up. He was, a little.

Mary changed her mind a dozen times as she gradually came to understand God's plan for her. She didn't become a lawyer or a missionary; she didn't marry Jerry; she didn't do a lot of things. If someone asked her now, she would see God's will in her marriage to Scott, but she probably couldn't see much beyond that. She will try many more things during her life. She will change her mind many times, too (but not about Scott). God's plan for Mary or anyone else often seems like an endless series of yes and no decisions.

The pattern for Kathy Benton was much the same. After she decided not to stay with her business-machine training and her city life, she did stay with college and her biology major, but she gave up being a hermit. More and more she found she needed the companionship of her friend John Mulligan. Their romance grew on them so gently that they were on the road to marriage months before either of them knew it.

Change is so much a part of our high-speed modern society that we almost take it for granted. It is almost 25 years since I finished college. During that time I have attended one seminary and one university, been pastor of five churches, and taught at four church colleges and one university. Now I spend about half my time remodeling run-down houses.

What I learned over those years is that, for each new challenge, many things have to be left behind. I have exchanged a dozen jobs for others. My family has moved more than a dozen times and more than 10,000 miles. Everyone in our family has left friends and opportunities behind. There have been times when doing what I thought was God's way for *my* life didn't seem the best for our children; there have also been times when I made choices that probably weren't God's first choices for me. We are all in hot pursuit of God's plan, but there is pain as well as pleasure in the search.

The time comes for all of us to make decisions to stay or go, to keep the job or quit it, to continue with school or stop, to get married or not.

There will be unwise decisions, wrong directions, side roads that lead off of God's way. The beauty of faith in Christ is that he goes with us, even down the side roads. It isn't long until we hear him whispering, "This is all wrong for you. Look here, I have a new plan."

At this point we may be reluctant to change, to backtrack, to admit we made a mistake. We may be terribly afraid. When we must face vocational changes, new options, new opportunities, *fear is the enemy*. As God's child and Christ's sister or brother, your every move, your every option and choice is monitored by your Lord. Caution is wise, but fear of the unknown path ahead may simply be lack of faith. If we all required that our vision of the road ahead be clear, no one would ever leave home, no one would ever change jobs, no one would ever get married.

Day-by-day faith in Jesus Christ brings awareness that he continually guides us toward our most productive pathways. Our faith in Christ and our openness to the Spirit's leading help us with those hundreds of yes and no decisions that finally determine God's way and our way through life.

CONCLUSION

Mary Laurence stepped into Pastor Anderson's office and gave him a big smile. "Is what my secretary tells me true?" he asked. Mary's smile became even broader as she nodded. "It is true, then. Scott Elstad! I didn't even know you were dating."

"We have been. Almost two years now."

"Tell me about yourself, Mary. You finished college, and then what did you do? Your mother told me some of it, but I guess I forgot."

As Mary spoke, Pastor Anderson thought back to that day, years before, when she sat crying in this same chair, wondering what to do with her life. She was a girl then, a bewildered girl.

As he listened to Mary's story, he began to nod and smile, too. "She's a woman now," he thought. "She's ready to be married. She has a future full of hope. She thinks she sees her future clearly. No fear at all in her eyes. Her life won't be very much like she sees it now, but that won't matter.

101

She'll handle her future all right. She and Scott will have a good life together. I'm sure they will."

Mary finished the account of her last several years and sat quietly for a moment. "Do you remember," she asked, "when I came in here all upset because I didn't know what to do?"

"Indeed I do. I was just thinking of it."

"I'm kind of ashamed when I think of that day. I was such a child."

"You were much younger and much less mature. You seem to have things well in hand now."

"I'm having an easier time making decisions. It's nice to have Scott. We talk things over for hours. We argue sometimes, too."

"That's good. No one can be happily married without arguing." Mary laughed and Pastor Anderson smiled at her. He couldn't get over the changes a few years had brought. "You know, Mary, I wish I'd had a crystal ball on my desk when you came in here years ago, crying and afraid. I could have said to you then, 'Look into this crystal ball, Mary, and see yourself six or seven years from now.' If you could have seen yourself as you look now, your worries would have been over."

"Do I really look that sure of myself?"

"Yes, you do. You look like you're on top of the world."

"I'm sure not as mixed up as I was in high school, but I'm still pretty scared—about marriage, I mean."

"That's what we're going to talk about, you and I and your Scott." He pulled his calendar book out of his pocket. "Now when could the three of us get together?"

102

Mary's faith held her together and kept her going when her plans were not yet formed. She made many mistakes and poor choices, but her faith helped her through them toward what God had intended all along. She has become and is still becoming the young woman God intended from the time of her birth. She has been looking primarily after herself as she was growing up and getting her training. She still has to look after herself, but she will soon have a husband and maybe even children. She will begin to take deeper interest in her neighbors and her friends, too. She has become, and is becoming, a servant.

There is no crystal ball. There's no way you or anyone else can see into the future. But there is a way to make that future more bright and promising, and that is to build on your Christian faith. "I have plans for you," God says, "plans for good and not for evil."

Believing and living that truth will root out much fear and make your choices about jobs, school, and marriage much easier in the next few years. God bless you in your deciding and in your living. It's a flawed world we live in, and we are flawed people—but life is exciting and challenging, and often rollicking fun for servants of Jesus Christ.